No Secrets:
Conversations with God

No Secrets:

Conversations with God

by

Dorothy Boone Kidney

Beacon Hill Press of Kansas City
Kansas City, Missouri

Quotations from the *New International Version of the New Testament*
(NIV), © 1973 by the New York Bible Society International. Used by per-
mission.

Foreword

Is God relevant? Is He concerned about us? Can we communicate with Him? Or He with us? This irreverent, careless age would say no—well, almost no, for men still cry out to Him when things go drastically awry.

One step up from ignoring God is to be casual about Him, and that too can be just about as blasphemous. But this attitude does point in the right direction for it is a healthy antidote for the opposite extreme—thinking of an autocratic God, remote and austere. For though His judgments are certain, and the sense of awe must never be lost, His love and mercy overshadow all His dealings with mankind. He is "out to get us," but only in the sense of drawing us to himself. Jesus came to bridge that gap.

God is not far off! He is concerned! He has told us to cast all our care upon Him for He cares for us. He is a loving God—not One to be formally addressed but One to converse with, to fellowship with, to commune with. Anytime, all the time the communication line is up. He wants us to share with Him our innermost feelings and our deepest concerns. Not that He does not know us altogether, but we need to open ourselves to Him.

It is this sense of intimacy which our author so aptly portrays in these encounters with God. May they serve to lead us all to richer and more meaningful experiences in prayer and communion with our Heavenly Father.

—J. FRED PARKER
Book Editor

*They that worship him
must worship him in spirit
and in truth.*

—John 4:24

It's not easy to be honest with You, God. To be completely frank and open. It's so much easier for me to pray for the missionaries, to ask You to "help the pastor today" and to bless all the little children than it is for me to tell it "like it is" in my own soul. I'm a bit ashamed to admit the hostile feeling I had about that woman I met this morning or to confess that I found the Sunday morning service a little boring.

I find myself often stepping out around a few unpleasant things in my morning prayer. Shame on me—forgive me. Perhaps I feel if I don't look too closely at my faults, they might go away! Help me to stop this ostrich-like habit in my prayers—praying about matters I feel are pleasing to You, but hiding my head in the sand and sidestepping the shameful part of me.

Help me to be *honest,* Lord—no secrets buried within. Help me to be open with You, no matter how humiliating or difficult.

So Nana's house is to be sold—the house of warm recollections of molasses cookies, the sewing machine with the two secret compartments, the small, familiar bedrooms, the cupboards that held the pretty dishes. I hang on so firmly, Lord, to things of the past. Somehow I cannot seem to bear the thought today that the familiar setting of my childhood is going to belong to strangers.

I want to gather all the sentimental treasures, the cozy relics, the heartwarming reminders around myself. I want everything to remain the same. But this is impossible. Sentimental attachments must give way to other people's plans, and I am left clutching a few tattered fourth-grade valentines, a chipped, flowered cream pitcher, a photograph of my grandmother's face.

O Lord, help me to divorce myself from the past—to remember that I must live in the important now. Reconcile me to the fact that loved ones must die, that friends do move away, and houses that hold special meaning for me cannot be mine forever. Help me, Lord, today because I find it hard to let go.

It's about time that I realized, Lord, that I am never going to be president of the United States, reach the moon, or be elected Outstanding Citizen of the Year. Not that I am striving for any of these great accomplishments, Lord, but I must learn to get my pleasures from the *little* things of life—the three yellow birds that sat on my wild cherry bushes yesterday, the gulls' white flight against the blue sky, my neighbor's crocuses today, and little Robbie's quick laugh Sunday.

Help me to savor the little things.

And thank You for giving me sight and the awareness to appreciate them.

Others-conscious," that's my greatly-needed key for the new year, Lord. Conscious of others and their needs. Spotlight off me. Christ at the core. The hub. With genuine spokes radiating in all directions. These are pretty phrases on paper on this first day of the new year. But not so easy to carry out. Impossible to carry out on my own. Fact acknowledged.

So infuse me with otherness, with real interest—not a put on interest. I'll do the yielding (and likely the "mistaking," as I so often do), but I'll *try* to stay yielded. *You* do the radiating. Not a big wheel anymore, Lord, help me to be a small circle of Christian love—motivated by Your wisdom and power.

It seems incredible, Lord, that she simply and quietly hired a U-Haul truck, backed it up to her own door, loaded on her personal belongings, and drove off—leaving a note for a surprised husband to find on his return from work! I didn't know her, Lord—just met her once briefly—but she seemed like such a tiny, timid person to go off like that clear across the nation.

I can't get her out of my mind. I wonder what long chain of events prompted her to do a thing like that. What brand of unhappiness was pushing her?

To be truthful, Lord, I think all of us at some time or other have felt like calling the U-Haul company on some rainy Monday morning. *You* know *I* have *thought* about it, Lord—and love for husband and family seems to have very little to do with it on those gloomy mornings. I guess it's the coward in us, Lord. I wonder how many people admit to having that leave-it-all-behind feeling. But we do stay on and in time You always do iron out the wrinkles, the rankles, and the momentary despair. Somehow You manage to shine through the mist strongly enough to help us count our blessings.

But all day I've thought of her, with her clothing, her sentimental treasures and few choice pieces of furniture stashed in the back of a U-Haul, climbing the mountains in the rain with windshield wipers going full blast, racing over the crowded highways, passing the sleeping villages at night with her thoughts in turmoil.

Be with her. Ride the seat beside her. I know nothing about her husband. But in his house where footsteps echo, be with him too tonight.

It just occurred to me today that it doesn't so much matter what we *look* like on the outside as what kind of person we are on the *inside*. It seems as if we *strive* so hard, Lord, to reach multiple, unrealistic goals. We strive for the gracious poise of celebrities, the chic appearance of a favorite friend, the intelligence of the panelists on a quiz show.

We want our houses to resemble homes in *House Beautiful,* we strive to make our dinner parties as superb as those in a gourmet restaurant, and try to have hairdos and faces as flawless as cover girls. But today, terribly belatedly I confess, I realized that people often feel insecure in the presence of such *perfection.* Instead, they feel more comfortable, relaxed, and happy in the presence of warm love. That is the essential requirement, and You showed me that today in 1 Corinthians 13: *Love is kind. . . . It is not proud. . . . It is not self-seeking. . . . It always protects, always trusts. . . . The greatest of these is love* (NIV).

Help me, Lord, to be more loving and kind, and less of a perfectionist.

Oh, I felt smug when I overheard the two women gossiping about Sandra! Yes, smug! I patted myself on my haloed shoulder and murmured to myself (like the purr of a contented kitten), "I, being a Christian, would not say those things about her; I would not gossip!" I felt so *proud* of my spiritual progress, my advanced state of grace. *"The Pharisee stood and prayed thus with himself, God, I thank thee, that I am not as other men are, extortioners, unjust, adulterers, or even as this publican"* (Luke 18:11).

Lord, humbly I want to make a trade. I want to trade that precious, Pharisaical robe I wrapped so elegantly around myself for a length of marked-down sackcloth! Shame on me! The sin of smugness, of spiritual pride, of haughty superiority was worse than the gossip.

I'm sorry, Lord. Genuinely sorry.

I could pray, "Lord, help me to grow old gracefully." But the fact is, Lord, I do not want to grow old at all. I think it would be rather nice to live to the end of my life being *this* age—or, better still, to lop off, say, about 30 years! This I know You won't do.

So what can I pray, Lord, except "Help me to grow old gracefully!" But I *do* ask, Lord, that You keep my *mind* young and alert, receptive to new ideas and fresh insights.

Help me to *relax*, Lord. I am assuming too much responsibility for the *outcome* of things! I am depending on my own will to the point of forgetting that You are in there plugging away on this project with me. I'm trying to prop You up, Lord, and steady Your hand. I guess I feel You need help from me to make this joint project a success.

Help me to rest—not to withdraw *all* my effort, but help me to lose my tenseness in the realization that our wills are united in this matter—that it's a partnership plan and that I'm not solely in charge!

This riddle that is Jennifer, Lord! How do I solve her? Or do I leave the solving to You? She used to be such an eager, active Christian and now she is leading an inconsistent life. And she does not seem to care that she has turned her back on You, that she is dabbling in the bright, false colors of life. Our conversations boomerang, limp, stagger, retreat, or stand still. We get nowhere, this once close friend and I. How can she so openly trample the good life, so publicly deny You?

O Lord, give me compassion, patience, and understanding. Help me to lift, not condemn; encourage and not judge. And in the meantime, Lord, talk to her in *Your* way —Your direct, un-boomeranging way—Your ever-kind but firm way. Please solve the Jennifer riddle and put together again the complicated pieces of her jigsaw life!

It's time to paint the fence, to spade the garden and to store the storm windows in the garage for another year.

It's a good time for repairing the loose shutter. For pounding nails. For sawing boards. For building an addition to the porch.

While I am swinging this hammer today (and missing the nail every third swing!), I am remembering You, Lord, the Carpenter whose hands once felt the smoothness of fine wood but which one day carried a rough cross. A God-Carpenter with His feet in the shavings, His head in the stars, and love in His heart. A Carpenter who made a yoke for oxen and, because He was God, could say, "Take my yoke upon you, and learn of me; for I am meek and lowly in heart: and ye shall find rest unto your souls. For my yoke is easy, and my burden is light" (Matt. 11:29-30). A God-Carpenter whose hands built a piece of farm equipment and whose blood built a highway to heaven!

I find spring is a good time, Lord. A good time for building . . . for remembering . . . for being grateful!

Lord, I wonder if the multitudes ever annoyed You. When they pushed and thronged about You, jammed You to the wall, did Your patience ever grow thin?

No, I don't suppose Your patience grew thin—You being divine. But being human as well as divine, perhaps You felt the stress, and the temptation to yield to impatience.

But, O Lord, sometimes the multitudes really get to me! The women in the supermarket who block the meat counters with their shopping carts making it impossible to get close enough to inspect the meat; the unbearably slow woman at the check-out counter holding up the whole line while she chats at great length with the girl at the register —all the while ineffectually pawing through an impossibly cluttered purse in an interminable search for her billfold!

The traffic jam at the intersection I can take, even being packed in too tightly in a small elevator with a man reeking of garlic breathing in my face, but oh, Lord, the line crashers, the shrill voices in a crowded room, the fight for space in a department store crowd at Christmas-time!

O Jesus, forgive me for looking through this glass so darkly, for misreading the road signs, for forgetting at times the reason I'm here—to love others, to see beyond the push of massed bodies to the harried, fearful, and sometimes desperately unhappy souls within those bodies. And thank You for money in my billfold to *buy* meat, for the *legs* that enable me to stand and wait for the slow woman at the check-out counter.

Give me an understanding heart and love to *see* the contemporary woman at the well, the Nathanaels of today under the fig tree, Lydia the seller of purple on the corner of Oak and Main streets, the sick man at the pool, and the desperate woman reaching for the hem of Your garment in the thickly packed crowds of this year in which I live.

I know, Lord, that the Bible urges us to use hospitality without grudging. Just yesterday I ran across the scripture which advises us to be "lovers of hospitality." But oh, Lord, I'm so *tired* tonight. There have been so many people visiting us in this summer cottage! Meals and meals and dishes and dishes—and everyone cooped up inside today because it rained! My hospitality has sprung a slow leak, Lord. I am weary and my smile is forced.

Help me, Lord, to be genuine in my hospitality. Right now I'm manufacturing a cheerful, you-are-welcome attitude. Help this Martha who is cumbered about with much serving.

I'd like to run away—far, far away tonight. Someplace quiet. Is there any place that's quiet anymore? Well, quiet me on the inside at least and help me to love everybody—even when it rains and I stumble over people's feet on my trips between stove and refrigerator.

Somebody upset my box of animal crackers. Somebody bumped into me, Lord, and sent my ice-cream cone splashing to the sidewalk.

That's what it amounts to, Lord. I thought it was an earth-shattering catastrophe at the time, but now that I am quiet and alone, I realize that my attitude was childish, the matter was very trivial after all. Help me to stop building these small, insignificant situations with childish blocks, then dissolving into tears when a careless foot knocks them to the ground.

Help me to be realistic, mature. Help me to cool it.

I need the *constant indwelling* of the Holy Spirit. I need the kind of emotional stability He can give, the mature approach to life situations that He provides.

Help me to refrain from hugging my teddy bear in great disappointment over small things, help me to discard the choo-choo train of always wanting my own way, help me to share my closely guarded little box of treasured marbles.

Help me to grow in maturity, Lord.

Lord, today I am remembering Joe Peterson, that eighth-grader, on the first day of school. I had asked each student to stand, introduce himself, to tell what he did during the summer and to state his hobby. When it became Joe's turn, he climbed heavily to his feet and announced, "My name is Joe Peterson; I didn't do nuthin' this summer, and I ain't got no hobby."

For some reason I have been thinking about Joe's honest but almost tragic report today. I wonder how many of us, like Joe, when facing You and on being asked how we spent the summer of our lives on this earth are going to say, "I didn't do nuthin', and I ain't got no hobby!"

I know, Lord, that my full-time occupation and "hobby" should be the winning of souls, helping others, and living for You. I know I do not have time to waste just "doin' nuthin'."

Help me to work consistently for You every day, to do the task at hand as You would have me do it. You reminded me today in Matt. 9:37 that "the harvest truly is plenteous, but the labourers are few." Please help me, Lord, to make good use of my time!

Tomorrow I really must try to go see Sadie. She is alone, lonely and needy. She is one of the multitude Jesus meant when He said to His disciples, "I have compassion on the multitude" (Matt. 15:32). And I must take something to her—a small Christmas present (a bit late because I have been away). But mostly I must take to her those things that Jesus would take to her if He were here on earth—love, interest, understanding—compassion.

BITS

Pieces and patchwork—
This is my life
Strewn on the floor
Of everyday living.

Fragments and tatters—
May they be joined
To make up a tapestry
Fit for the heavens.

Odd bits and remnants
Haphazardly dropping
Through the small hours
Of every day.

Prayers, and pie baking,
Sick calls, and mending,
Bright sunny patches
Mixed in with the gray.

Fashioning colors,
Working out detail,
Weaving a pattern
Too varied to see.

Cross-stitch and backstitch,
Slow, quiet, steady—
Assortment of pieces
All falling together.

Making my tapestry,
Knitting my afghan
Out of the broken
Snatches of life.

Days from the hours,
Years from the blending—
O Lord, may it mean something
When it is finished!

Sometimes it seems to me, Lord, that nothing lives up to its beginnings. I have had so many excitement-crammed beginnings which, given enough time, have fizzled out into low-burning, dying sputters like final gasps of Fourth-of-July firecrackers.

I never pass that gray, square school building but I remember how I charged into that teaching situation fired with enthusiasm, bursting at the seams with anticipation, only to have enthusiasm gasp its last breath during a series of sicknesses that forced my resignation from teaching.

Then, before that, there was the new house. All that fresh paint and gorgeous, new wallpaper! I unrolled the 9 x 12 braided rug and everything was "coming up roses." I was perched excitedly again on the threshold of another "new beginning." But after the house was completed, loneliness set in and I couldn't see the fresh paint around that dark cloud of loneliness—and we sold the house.

I know You must be displeased with me today for reshuffling and counting up these "beginnings turned to disappointments," especially since You have given me so *many* great blessings in life, but somehow it helps me to spread out this series of letdowns. Help me, Lord, not to place so much importance on beginnings, not to *expect* so much of them.

Honestly, Lord, today I feel that the only beginning that *doesn't* disappoint us through the test of time is the "new birth." I am glad it hasn't fizzled out, and although there have been a few disappointments along the way, the end (eternal life in heaven) is going to be even better than the beginning. Thank You for the permanence and continued blessings of the new birth!

I thank You today for the knowledge and engineering skill You gave Alexander Graham Bell, Thomas Edison, the Wright brothers, and Henry Ford.

I thank You for the intelligence and curiosity You gave Joseph Lister, Madame Curie, and other scientists through the years.

This car I drive, Lord, is such a marvelous convenience. And I thank You for the hot water that gushes from the faucet, the light switch on the wall, my automatic oven, my frostless refrigerator, and the jet that takes me from here to there so quickly.

I thank You for antibiotics when I am sick, for the doctors' medical knowledge, the surgeons' skill.

I am so blessed today with conveniences, luxuries, and comforts, that I feel like mingling a plea for forgiveness along with my prayer of thanks. When I compare my way of life with less fortunate people in the world, I feel humble, unworthy, but deeply grateful. I do not deserve these manifold blessings, but I do thank You. You are so good and thoughtful.

I even thank You today for the vacuum cleaner I hate to have to push over the floors and for that old, faulty, temperamental toaster that either burns the toast to a crisp or toasts it to an unsatisfactory dry tan!

I thank You, Lord, for letting me *reach* this birthday, for giving me rich, grace-filled years, for watching over me, protecting me, guiding me, for picking me up when I have fallen.

I thank You for friends made along the way, for years of answered prayers, for happy experiences, for days of beauty and nights of restful sleep.

You are my special Gift on this birthday. I thank You for yourself.

Would You believe that I'm not begging for something in this prayer? Well, I'm not. Do You feel this is a welcome change, Lord? Likely You do.

I want to say thank You for the elm tree growing near my window, for my friend Lois with the good advice, for water rushing in the gutter this spring day, for love, for yourself, for life, for the Bible. And I thank You for the river, the bright stars last night, the jonquils which are blooming near the house. And the eyes with which to see it all!

My heart responds to the words of the Psalmist today: "Blessed be the Lord, who daily loadeth us with benefits, even the God of our salvation" (68:19). For indeed, Lord, You *load* us with benefits, and *daily* at that! I marvel that You have given us the benefit of daily communication with You, the benefit of the daily atonement, the benefit of a clear mind, of the indispensable Bible. And on top of these—family, friends, eyesight, hearing, ability to work, to walk, to play.

These benefits are more important than the wall-to-wall shag rug and the electric dishwasher. Those are unnecessary luxuries, but the spiritual gifts are the all-important parts of my life. And You give them not sparsely, reluctantly, in a limited way, but You *load* us with them—*daily!* As the teenagers say, "Wow!" Thank You, Lord, for Your abundant generosity!

I walked into the world this morning, Lord, and found it a big, empty room. People were meaningless shadows. Love and comfort were simply words one looked up in the dictionary. Loneliness was real. Sadness had meaning. All other words were lost on me. It was as if You had set my feet on a vast, uninhabited globe to stumble around by myself. And I felt if I should cry out, all I would hear would be the echo of my own voice bouncing off the Rocky Mountains, crashing across the Grand Canyon and slamming against the sheer cliffs of ice in Antarctica.

Where are You, Lord, this wide, blank day? *People* are here but I cannot touch them; they touch me but their touch is like the impersonal brushing of a tree branch against my face or an indifferent gust of wind ruffling my hair slightly—very slightly.

I walk alone and no one reads my thoughts. I smile and say, "Lovely day, Mrs. Brown," to the lady in front of the laundromat. The *surroundings* are beautiful but the day is a misty nothing. Life is a riddle I cannot decipher.

Faith has disintegrated to far less than a mustard seed. Somewhere inside me I am tired. Everywhere inside me I am tired.

Jesus, did You have days like this?

This meaningless void. I have forgotten all the lessons I have learned, have misplaced the key, have somehow smudged my glasses, the road signs have all blown away.

I grope.

Zero in on me, Lord, and renew my perspective. It's a cold wind that blows today.

The scriptures remind me that "even the winds and the sea obey him." Let the wind of the Holy Spirit blow on me, Lord—not the frightening wind that crashed against the disciples as they cried in the storm, "Lord, save us: we perish!"

Reach out Your hand and right the road signs, steady me. I cannot walk this desert alone today.

Such a magnificent, perfect, super-terrific answer to prayer, Lord! The answer came so swiftly, so surely, so "just-rightly"! You are so amazing! And Your timing is superb!

I *float* today. I simply float on this cloud of praise. Indeed You hear. Indeed You answer. Oh, indeed You do! Sometimes Your affirmative or negative answer comes after a long period of time but today Your answer came so quickly!

I pray for an hour over something. Then when the answer comes, I say "Thank You" in a brief one-minute prayer, but it does not mean that my gratefulness is any less. Thank You, Lord, thank You for such a quick, visible, spectacular answer to prayer today!

He spoke my name outside the dark tomb
Of my shadowed past.

He reached out His hand in the glorious sunshine
Of my personal Easter.

> *He spoke my name.*
> *One word.*
> *But I heard,*
> *Maybe because I had been listening*
> *For my name spoken in just that way*
> *For a long time,*
> *A long, long time.*

It was all there in my spoken name—
The compassion, the understanding, the love,
The forgiveness.

Especially the forgiveness.

A new me emerged from the shadows,
Shining and alive,
On my personal Easter!

"Because I live, ye shall live also" (John 14:20).

Take the *hurry* out of me, Lord. I seem to rush about so—bodily, mentally, emotionally. The scripture "Be still and know that I am God" is such an elusive thing for me today. I need stillness for my soul—an island of quiet in the thrashing activities of this day. Running I get nowhere. Hurrying I fall behind. In the multitude of so many things to do I feel tense, hurried. Unwind me, Lord. Insulate me against fretting.

Did *You* rush about like this when You were on earth? Was *Your* life jumbled discord? I don't believe it was.

In frantic hurry there is confusion.

Un-confuse me, Lord. Un-tense me. Help me to sort the trivial from the important. And speak to the waters of my soul, "Peace, be still!" I invite You to stand up in the small, tossing boat of my life, Lord, and calm the raging wind and sea today.

It's hard not to look back, Lord, at the ruined years. At night especially, the wrecked years return to haunt me. Most of the time I can function as if those wasted years never existed; other times by a definite control of will I ignore them. But on a sleepless night, such as tonight, they skulk back into my thoughts, laden with heartbreak, as sharp and as real as if there had been no interlude of time between the *then* and *now*.

Going backward in thought is such a waste, Lord. To resurrect an unhappy, forgiven past, to bring to life again the old ghosts, to drag rattling skeletons out of their musty closets, to rake over the ashes, to open the wounds, to peer into dark caverns where thousands of tears have been shed is so useless. And yet, tonight my mind reverts, plays again the time-weary cassettes, flicks the better-to-be-forgotten pictures again across my mental screen.

I am worn out with remembering, yet my mind dredges it all up, the hours tick by and I cannot sleep. I try to fortify myself with scripture. I lean hard for a few minutes on Paul's admonition, "Forgetting those things which are behind, and reaching forth unto those things which are before, I press toward the mark for the prize of the high calling of God in Christ Jesus."

Then my thoughts zero in on the frightening scripture, "But if ye forgive not men their trespasses, neither will your Father forgive your trespasses."

O Lord, I did forgive. I do forgive. I forgive everyone. I forgive myself. Forgive me. It is three o'clock in the morning and my mind races with thoughts of forgiveness.

Are there any remnants of bitterness? "Search me, O God, and know my heart: try me, and know my thoughts. And see if there be any wicked way in me, and lead me in the way everlasting." Erase the bitterness if there *is* any bitterness—and if there is no bitterness, then erase the remaining sadness. Help me to refrain from looking in the rearview mirror.

It is four o'clock. Finally I sleep.

I awake to snow drifting in great, white flakes across my window. I stand looking at the incredible quietness and peace of the snow-laden elm trees.

Let peace infiltrate my soul, Lord. Let the white snow of forgiveness cover the jagged ruts and crooked scars. Cover with a white mantle my sin of reviewing it all last night. I thank You, Lord, for the blood of Jesus Christ, Your Son, that whitens and erases and cleanses from all sin. And now let me get at these dishes piled in the sink, at this floor that needs vacuuming. Amen.

I am glad, Lord, that You love and understand the many Marthas of this world—that You do not condemn us, despise us, or give up on us. Rather, You are always present to encourage us, to counsel us, to pick us up out of our dilemmas and to set us on our feet again.

Without You we could not function. Without You life would be a maze of unsolvable difficulties.

But life with You makes it possible to cope with the difficulties and with the uncertainties of life.

So thank You, Lord, for always listening—for BEING THERE, and for Your infinite patience and understanding.

I thought that gloxinia plant was finished, Lord! When it was blooming on Inez's windowsill, the blossoms were glossy and purple. But later I saw it on her porch, brown and dried-up. Then she put the poor, shriveled thing in a dark corner of her cellar. You must have smiled when I remarked to her, "That's the trouble with some plants; they just don't last!"

And You must have smiled even more when I saw a gorgeous gloxinia flowering on her windowsill and exclaimed, "You have another gloxinia! This one is a beauty!"

I was so embarrassed, Lord, when she explained, "No, it's the same old gloxinia. I brought it up from the cellar." Then she patiently explained to me the mystery-surprise of a gloxinia—that, after a period in a dark place, it will thrive and bloom again if placed in the sunlight. She certainly has the glowing purple evidence of that miracle right there in her kitchen!

Today, Lord, I'm thinking that Christians often are like Inez's gloxinia plant. Sometimes we reach periods when we are set aside momentarily in a shadowed place— a loved one dies, we lose our job, are sick or discouraged. Like the gloxinia plant, we look almost licked—the life seems to be nearly gone out of us. "Valley times" I believe You called them in Your Word, God. The cellar times. The dark periods.

You know I've experienced those times, Lord. There was one especially dark time, but You were there in the darkness. And after You brought me out of that darkness, there was a richness and a beauty which I had never before experienced. It seemed as if my life became deeper, fuller, even more fruitful, because of that "cellar experience" with You.

I'm glad, Lord, that You promised to walk with us through all circumstances of life. Today I am especially grateful for Your Word which promises: "When thou passest through the waters, I will be with thee; and through the rivers, they shall not overflow thee: when thou walkest through the fire, thou shalt not be burned; neither shall the flame kindle upon thee" (Isa. 43:2).

Thank You for answering prayer and for clearing up some of my guilt by showing me there are two sides to a coin! Do You remember how terrible I felt because I was showing hospitality so grudgingly that rainy day in our summer camp? (Of course, You remember! That's a tremendous thought, Lord—that You always remember, that Your memory is never faulty!)

You allowed me to bump into another scripture relevant to hospitality yesterday. *"Withdraw thy foot from thy neighbour's house; lest he be weary of thee, and so hate thee"* (Prov. 25:17).

So the *guest* has a responsibility too, Lord—just as much as the hostess! Help me, Lord, never to overstay my visits in other people's homes and by doing so, wear out my welcome!

Verily I say unto you, Wheresoever this gospel shall be preached in the whole world, there shall also this, that this woman hath done, be told for a memorial of her" (Matt. 26:13).

Wheresoever this gospel shall be preached in the *whole world!* Lord, I know You meant in today's world, too (a much *larger* world than the known world at the time this was written). And how much bigger the population figure is today! This woman's act of anointing Your head with ointment is *still* being told as You prophesied. This one act really "made waves," to use today's vernacular, Lord—far-reaching waves, a whole domino-row of reactions tumbling headlong through all the years, a chain reaction of influence reaching lives even in *this* generation!

What simple act of mine done for You today can set up a chain reaction for good, Lord? Can I touch one life, say one word of encouragement, bind up a wound beside the busy freeway?

I offer You the ointment of my day. As for the memorial, Lord, I crave none. I believe she craved no recognition either. Love for You is the motivating force.

There has to be a song in it somewhere for me, Jesus. In religion, I mean. There has to be something in it that will *do* something for me, and *make* something of me. I need a song, an inspiration, a gentle push, a tender touch, a listening ear, and a force to pull me up and set me going each day of the week. It has to be a "middle-of-the-week" religion and not just the Sunday kind, because often I bog down in the middle of the week. I have troubles seen and unseen. I need someone to take care of me who knows what's what. Someone I can talk to even if I live all alone up on Codohootoots Mountain with my nearest neighbor 10 miles away.

It has to be what someone has called an "every moment, thriving, realistic, Lord-and-me relationship." And I'm glad it's all present in this new life-style You gave me after I met the conditions. I am glad I met You, Jesus—the One who wrote down the facts, set down the conditions, and made the relationship available. For in You I have found the song and all the other necessary ingredients—plus eternal life.

For these great gifts I thank You!

Jesus, thank You for healing the bruises of my soul—the invisible-to-the-human-eye bruises which I have received in the battering waves of life.

Thank You for *seeing* the bruises, Lord. No one else knew they were there, but You are healing them.

Time is not the great healer, Lord—*You* are! For this I say, "Thank You!"

I am so glad, Lord, that You did not leave it up to me to choose my *own* way. You know how hopelessly snarled up I can get trying to get on and off freeways, and You remember the many times I have been lost in the woods. You know it takes me literally years to find my way around medium-sized cities every time we move, and I've even lost my way trying to locate my room in a hotel. Trying to decipher road maps is beyond my understanding and I never learned to read a compass.

So thanks, Jesus, for laying out the route for me so simply that even a child can understand. Surely You had me with my easily-confused-sense-of-direction in mind when You charted the course in the Bible and placed the road markers of a manger, a cross, and an empty tomb along the way. Thank You!

Buried somewhere in this problem I know there is a key.

How freely do You give out keys, Lord? Do You have a whole ring of jangling keys to hand out just for the asking? And *how* do You hand them to us? Through our own thoughts, the wisdom You have given us? Through thoughts prompted by the Holy Spirit? By a search of the Scriptures? By counseling with a trusted friend? Through prayer? Yes, all those ways. Certainly through prayer, I believe. Then searching the Scriptures, maybe counseling with a trusted friend—perhaps in that order?

This needle-in-the-haystack key! Help me to ferret it out, Lord. Otherwise, the problem remains locked.

Give me insight into the details of the problem, help me to utilize the ways You have given us in Your Bible so I may work this problem out through Your help and guidance.

Today help me to make a list of priorities, Lord. There are so many things I *must* do, so many activities I *want* to do, so many nagging jobs I'm going to *have* to do, so many errands I *should* do, so many tasks I *hate* to do, a few projects I really should *finish,* a couple of things that it seems I'll *never* get time to finish, and that new project I'd like to *get started on.*

Where do I start? What's the most important? How do I budget my time, my strength? What should I leave undone? Untangle my thoughts, Lord, and help me to separate the important from the trivial.

The lists go on and on—the meals must be prepared, the dishes washed, the buttons sewed on, the marketing done, the clothes taken to the cleaners. Milford asked me to get the oil changed in the car, I promised to speak this week at the Monday morning sharing group, and I have company coming tonight for dinner.

How do I get into these messes?

Would You bail me out please? Guide me as I prepare this priority list.

All right. I'll start with prayer—special, deep-thinking prayer. Then I'll read some portion from the Bible—not about the hurried Martha today, or impetuous Peter—maybe a psalm to calm me down or whatever passage You may lead me to.

Now that I've done that, my head seems clearer, my nerves steadier. Now the list.

I *must* feed my family, and certainly we can't eat from dirty dishes so—meal preparation and dishwashing. And I'll keep the menu for dinner tonight simple. I'll skip the grocery shopping and use what I have on hand. Push the button sewing and the hobby projects into another day. Arise early tomorrow morning to work on the devotional talk for the sharing group. Get the oil changed in the car, and while I'm out make a call on lonely Mrs. Loring in the convalescent home.

I'll not vacuum the floor for company, the clothes for the cleaner will have to wait until Saturday.

And in the middle of the afternoon I'll read some more stabilizing passages from the Bible. And, yes, I'll take a nap. Or try to. I'll need a nap by then. That should help.

Thank You, Lord, for unmuddling me, helping me to see things in true perspective. And help me, please, not to get so cluttered again; help me to live more *simply* and not to continue burying myself under mountains of tasks!

Just a few words to this church group are enough, Lord—if You are in those few words.

A torrent of words without You would be like an avalanche of nothing, a meaningless chant.

So be *in* the few words, Lord. Let them be strong, forceful, electrifying words. Break up "these few loaves of my devotional talk," Lord, and pass out pieces of it to all who are there—even as You did with the loaves on the grassy hillside—so all will be filled and none will go away hungry.

It's a curious thing, Lord, that the human voice by going up and down can make music—that even the birds have been given the right notes to create song. That music-thought was beautiful, Lord, and how much it has meant for all of us.

And I am so glad today that when You made colors that it occurred to You to make *pink*—and so many *shades* of pink! I marvel over the deep pink of azaleas, the pale pink of a baby's fingertips, and the glowing pink of sunsets. I enjoy that rosy-pink of my new sweater. Pink was such a good idea.

Laughter was brilliant, too. Such an unusual way to express happiness! Boy, we'd really feel confused and bottled-up if we didn't have laughter. Laughter was a great gift, Lord, and I thank You.

I guess tears have their place in the scheme of things, too. I'm quite sure that biting one's lip in extreme sorrow would not be so therapeutic as shedding tears. And even clapping one's hands to express great happiness could not quite take the place of tears of joy or tears of relief or even tears of deep affection.

The human body is simply great, Lord. The world You created is extremely beautiful, and the accessories of music, color, laughter, and tears add invaluable dimensions to our lives! Thank You!

I have always considered it strange that those two plaques on my bedroom wall have always disturbed me. "God Answers Prayer" one states; the twin to it (which I have hung directly under the other one) adds: "Prayer Changes Things."

Today—after week-long praying about a situation which has not changed—the reason for the uncomfortable feeling I have always had about that pair of plaques emerged clearly. I do not believe that You always *change* things in answer to prayer, as those wall mottoes state. I believe sometimes, instead, You change people so they can put up with things—so they can tolerate unchanged circumstances. *God answers prayer* and *prayer changes things* don't necessarily go together.

Help me to adjust to these circumstances I find myself in, Lord. Give me the "needed grace" to cope with the unchangeable. Remind me again that You have promised, "My grace is sufficient for thee: for my strength is made perfect in weakness. Most gladly therefore will I rather glory in my infirmities, that the power of Christ may rest upon me" (2 Cor. 12:9).

This kitchen, Lord. You know how disappointed I am. Somehow the renovation just didn't live up to those great expectations on paper! It's not a total disaster. But it falls short, far short, of what I had planned.

Wouldn't You think I'd learn not to expect so much of clay, wood, flesh, and bone? I expect so much of carpenters! And plumbers! And doctors! And friends! And family!

"There is none perfect but God." *You* said that, Jesus.

There is such a dearth of perfect things, Lord! Me included. Especially me.

If there are degrees of happiness in heaven, then I feel I'll be the happiest person there just because of the *perfection* of the place! I am so terribly let down on this earth when things are less than perfect. I naively go through life expecting perfection and am always shatteringly surprised to find that things (people, myself, and circumstances) are constantly lacking and falling far short of my expectations. Finding imperfections *over and over* jolts me *over and over.*

Well, anyway, moth and rust *will* corrupt and thieves will break in and steal (in time)—I mean all these "imperfect things," these material possessions. And Christian imperfections (due to lack of knowledge—and in my case, lack of good common sense!) will be made *perfect* up there, too.

I'm looking *forward,* Lord, to a perfect heaven. Up there I'll sing, with perfect pitch, a perfect song of perfect triumph.

The answer to my problem didn't come in quite the way I had expected, Lord. But it seems to be a most adequate answer.

You urged us through the Scriptures to *"Trust* in the Lord with *all* thine heart; and lean not unto thine own understanding. In *all* thy ways acknowledge him, and he *shall* direct thy paths" (Prov. 3:5-6). The italics are mine, Lord, but the truth is Yours, and that key word, "trust," especially impresses me. I have acknowledged You in all the ways I know, and although I do not understand *how* it's going to turn out, I'm trusting You. Trust is the key for me, Lord. Surely You know what You are doing. I'll keep on acknowledging and trusting *You* (and not my own understanding), and I *know* You will keep Your promise to direct my paths.

I realize You have other kinds of solutions for problems, but I feel for today at least the one You are leading me to is *trust.* I shall wait for You to show me the way.

Lord, as I was out shopping the other day for kitchen curtains, I was amazed to see a man running up an escalator which was going in the same direction he was! If he had only stood still, the escalator would have gotten him up to the second floor without his exerting any effort at all. But he was too impatient and wouldn't wait for the upward motion of the escalator to take him up.

Later on, Lord, I got to thinking about that man running up the escalator. I have been guilty at times of running up this moving escalator of life, too. Instead of standing still and allowing You to move me forward in Your will, with *Your power,* I have charged ahead, activated my body and raced my motor only to find later on that if I had stood still, I could have accomplished the mission with less effort and achieved the same result.

Help me to always remember that the powerful escalator of the Holy Spirit will move me along surely and forcefully if I obey Him and follow His timing. I know it's best not to run impatiently up Your escalator when You caution me, "Child, stand still." I know if I permit You to direct me, You will get me there in due time refreshed, confident, and not all out of breath as I usually am!

Thank You for directing me to the scripture today in which You made the same promise through Your servant Moses to the people: "Fear ye not, stand still, and see the salvation of the Lord, which he will shew to you to day" (Exod. 14:13).

I don't care much for bugs, Lord, but I must admit they are fascinatingly made. It looks as if You just twisted some bits of fine, dark thread together to make this one, and then gave him a few quick black strokes with Your delicate paint brush.

And that little bee over there on the flower is an incredible wonder! You gave him a buzz and a soft, bright "polo" coat. After buttoning the orange coat with its black stripes around him, You started his flying mechanism, threw the switch to start the buzzing motor, and sent him off with instructions for making honey.

I get such a terrific bolt of faith watching the bee! He's such an intricate, energetic, little creature. All bundled up. Sound-equipped. An industrious employee of the Honey Manufacturing Corporation—worldwide—manufacturing honey, cross-pollinating plants everywhere, with You acting as Supervisor and President.

I realize that the bee is a very small part of Your "large-scale" universe. But You have a well-defined plan for even a small buzzing insect. Watching this bee today, I am very much aware that You are a God of plans with directions to be followed.

I know You give each of us instructions to follow, the necessary physical and mental abilities to understand the instructions, and You set us off on a course to carry out Your plans, even as You did the bee.

Help me today, Lord, to follow my detailed blueprint as carefully as this busy, buzzing bee follows his!

When I reach heaven, Lord, I'd like to have a gathering of friends whom I have not met yet personally. Some afternoon I'd like to invite them over for tea and celestial cookies.

I'd like to invite Martha. I think I'd like Martha. She and I have shared so much in common on our earthly pilgrimages. And it would be nice if she'd bring her sister Mary. I can learn so much from Mary. Perhaps Sarah will relate to me some of her experiences as a busy mother. And I'm anxious to talk to Lydia, that seller of purple fabric. I was never a successful businesswoman, but You know I enjoy talking with women who lead enthusiastic, busy, business lives.

And Priscilla, Aquilla's wife! She'd be delightful, I'm sure. They sound like such a nice couple, taking time from their days of tentmaking to tell their generation about You. I certainly plan to invite Leah. I have always felt sorry for her. I know she will be happy in heaven, but I'd like her to know that I sympathized with her. And Rachel must have been pretty. I want to invite her, too—although she'll have a celestial body in heaven I know. And I'd like to invite the woman at the well. I've often wondered what her name was.

And Your earthly mother, Jesus—I especially want to meet her! I've always admired her so. Peter's mother-in-law will receive an invitation. We can compare notes—how it felt to be touched by Your miraculous hand and healed of sickness. I'm going to ask Dorcas to teach me to sew. I've never learned down here; I'm all thumbs. Maybe I could ask Rhoda, too. I really learned very little about her in the Bible, except that she went to the door when Peter knocked after his release from jail and ran in her excitement back into the room without opening the door. I've always felt she was a teenager then. I'd like to meet her.

I'm looking forward to it! It will be, I am sure, one of the best women's sharing groups I have ever attended.

That Rock was Christ" (1 Cor. 10:4). Thank You, God, for that Rock! Stronger than cement! Bigger than a skyscraper! Sturdier than a mountain! Firmer than steel!

I need a Rock today—a Rock I can fling myself onto with no danger of its collapsing into the swirling hours of this unstable afternoon. I need something solid under me, Lord, to keep these greedy, reaching waves from sweeping me out to an impossible sea.

No shifting, slippery sand for me today. I need a great, strong, dependable, safe, immovable Rock!

Right now I rest my tired self, with all its tension and cares, onto Your sure strength. Then later I'll return to the busy hours of this day rested and refreshed, stilled by Your calmness, relaxed in Your greatness and Your always-thereness.

Help me to keep away from that jar of peanut butter, Lord, and that can of peanuts! They are so calorie-laden and I enjoy that peanutty taste so much! We're familiar with that pattern, You and I; I nibble and gain weight, grow depressed because I'm overweight, nibble some more because I'm depressed, gain more weight, become more depressed and so on. And last week when I hit that all-time low, overweight despondency, I sneaked out and ordered that hot fudge sundae with all those nuts. I'm so ashamed of my lack of willpower and that huge, hot fudge sundae.

So help me please to resist the peanut butter jar, the jar of cookies, and the luscious cake my neighbor brought in. Help me to close my eyes when I walk by that picture of a sundae in the drugstore window.

"Feed me with food *convenient* for me." I found that verse in the 30th chapter of Proverbs, Lord, the eighth verse. The problem is, Lord, that stupid peanut butter jar is just too convenient, too handy. I know the word "convenient" in the scripture surely means "needful."

I thank You for providing the food needful for me. Strengthen my will to choose the food I require and not what I want. Help me to put *starch* in my willpower and not in my body.

Autumn has come to our small town. I feel as if I am wandering over a huge artist's palette, lost in a maze of tempera paints. Nature is having a color jubilee and I am giddy with fall, Lord. I walk under tall elms trailing their yellow streamers; I climb brown hills polka-dotted with orange flowers; I go to sleep under fall skies spiked with clear, crystal stars; and I walk over ordinary ground which has been transformed into a colorful afghan of leaves.

My own street is a crimson, gypsy scarf, and my feet on the leaf-strewn sidewalk are crackling red and orange songs.

If this breathtaking fall day is merely earth, Lord, oh, what will heaven be?

> *No eye has seen,*
>   *no ear has heard,*
> *no mind has conceived*
>   *what God has prepared for those*
>   *who love him* (1 Cor. 2:9, NIV).

So it turned out all right, Lord! After all that worry! Your hand surely winds the clock, turns the wheel, and presses all the right buttons. You whispered that one word: *trust*. So I did trust—a rather unusual feat for me, but I did trust. Actually I was calm about the whole thing, and it did work out.

Why can't I always be like that? Why do I go into such emotional tailspins and create great tizzies for myself when You are up there all the time at the control panel pushing the right buttons? I am a compulsive worrywart, a neurotic do-it-myself button-pusher, but there was a lesson to be learned there today. Wish I could learn it once —bang!—for all time, but I seem to have to relearn it, reapply it, to memorize it daily. I'm prone to forget it tomorrow!

Well, anyway, we scored a bull's-eye today! Maybe there's more than mere words wrapped up in that song that suggests, *"Trust* and *obey,* for there's no other way to be *happy* in Jesus, but to trust and obey!"

There have been some things in life which I have asked for that You haven't given me, Lord. Now, looking back on those times, I can understand that it was best for me not to receive them.

That farm I wanted to buy so badly! I can see now that the farmhouse would have been much too large for me to cope with.

And that job as social worker I so desperately wanted! Now that years have passed I can see good reasons why that particular job wouldn't have worked out for me.

There have been so many places in my life where, if I'd had my way, I would have taken attractive side roads, would have explored beckoning lanes, taken wrong turns, and blundered down blind alleys. I'm glad You *have* led me and have denied me those things that would have led me down unplanned highways.

I am completely immersed in the *present,* Lord, and I have no way of seeing around the curve in the road to the *future,* but as I look over my shoulder, the highway I have traveled makes sense. I know You view my future as easily as I view my past, and that You will guide me. For this I thank You!

What is your favorite holiday?" was the question asked in the newspaper this week.

"The Fourth of July," someone said.

Oh, Lord, the Fourth of July bigger than Christmas? Any day more favorite or more important than the day You were born?

Some of the people did name Christmas as their favorite holiday, but, Lord, for the most pathetic reasons, like snow, the excitement of purchasing and receiving gifts, vacations! But not one word about You, Jesus.

The colors red and green may signify only colors of gift paper and decorations to many people, but since I became a Christian, Lord, red suddenly has become very much the color of blood shed for me, and green the color of thorns that went to create a makeshift crown!

Easter is a big day, too, Lord. We can include that. I think Christmas and Easter should be very favorite. They should outshine all the holidays!

"What is your favorite holiday?" they asked in the local newspaper this week. And I fear the answers pushed the thorns a little deeper into Your forehead, Lord, and drove the spikes harder into Your hands!

Dear Lord, help me to rest in You. Help me to do my best in my labors for You and not to strain and push so hard at the job. Help me to remember that this is Your work and that You are the motivating force behind every task I attempt for You.

I realize that the work You give us to do should be done through *Holy Spirit calmness* and not through stressful, human strain, through fretting and anxiety. But sometimes I become so busy, so tense, so anxious that I feel driven in my thinking, rushed in my activities, and pushed beyond my endurance, even while working for You.

On this Labor Day may I learn the meaning of the verse which cautions us to "be still and know that I am God." Help me to remember that without Christ I can do nothing and in quietness and confidence shall be my strength. For I know that it is only through Christ's wisdom, guidance, and unfailing supervision that any job is accomplished successfully.

So Esley has died. Last night at 11:30.

His testimonies in prayer meetings during this last year have consisted mainly of reminiscing about "the good old days" when he was young and "working for the Lord." Through the years his testimonies have been spiced with hallelujahs. So for Esley now it is over.

I am in the "good old days" now—middle-aged but not bedridden. I'd hate to think I'm wasting these middle years on trivial things. I'm making my later-year memories now.

Lord, reach down for this prayer tonight. Let these years count for You. Vitally! Eternity-wise!

Time races!

Good night, Esley. We'll miss your hallelujahs.

I agree with the late Peter Marshall that what we need most these days is the God of the humdrum, the commonplace, the everyday. It's the everydayness, Lord, that really gets to me. I need You in my kitchen and while driving through traffic. I have to talk to You when I'm hung up and high up, and when I emerge battle-scarred at the end of a day.

I need You when I'm filled with great happiness and when someone has burst my shiny, new balloon. I need You when I look at this face in the mirror in the morning, when I burn the toast at breakfast, when I see little children suffering in the hospital, and when I can't get the car started. There is so much I don't understand, so much I love You for, so much I question You about, so much guidance and common sense I lack.

Oh, I need You, Lord, I need You! That's how the words of the song go—I need You every hour! And I am glad—glad—glad that You are there when I need You!

While cutting out a batch of cookies today, Lord, I found myself being thankful that You didn't use a cookie cutter when you made people. I'm glad You didn't stamp everyone out in the size and shape of uniform gingerbread men, but made us all different shapes and sizes—physically and personality-wise. You even frosted us differently—brown, yellow, and white.

And I'm glad You didn't use a *favorite* cookie recipe either to make one select batch of people—a master race—then throw the rest of us together following an inferior recipe. I'm glad You used the same, loving dough to make us all.

I'm glad today that we're not identical—as if rolled off Your creative assembly line. I'm glad that each person is unique and that You have given each the talent and aptitude suited to his own personality to use for Your glory.

Noontime. Lord, it was a partial lie—a half-truth if there is such a thing. The principal came into my classroom and asked if I had ever conducted a county spelling bee. I had once, but it had made me almost sick with worry and I had done a terrible job in front of principals, faculty, and the superintendent where I formerly taught. I was afraid I might be appointed right on the spot to conduct another one so I said, "Well, I have *participated* in them." Oh, Lord, I not only had participated, I *had* conducted them. He went over the material with me and did not ask me to *conduct* it. Now I feel guilty. I should have told the whole truth regardless of consequences. Forgive me. Help me not to become involved again in half-truths.

* * *

Now I have just learned that I am to be *in charge* of the county spelling bee after all! Well, Lord, give me the strength, time, and wisdom.

Help me to rearrange my thinking, Lord. I seem to have lost my sense of values. I have attached too much importance to my own happiness and have placed more value on *things* than on *people*. The price tags have become terribly askew. I am reaching unsuccessfully for the elusive ring on the merry-go-round for self, digging about the hills looking for my own personal pot of gold at the end of the rainbow, and even digging up the turf hunting for the impossible Fountain of Youth. I *know* happiness is not to be found in these selfish, blind alleys.

Help me to be more interested in others today and less interested in self. When Agnes comes bursting through the door and interrupts a piece of writing I am doing, help me to lay it aside graciously and visit with her happily. When Nora pours out her long list of daily troubles to me, help me to really listen and to help her. When other people's plans smash up my own plans, help me to be kind and yielding. Help me to willingly share my time, my self, and my energy with others.

The Psalmist wrote: "Be merciful unto me, O God: for man would swallow me up; he fighting daily oppresseth me" (56:1).

People swallowers! I have heard of sword-swallowers and goldfish swallowers but, apparently, Lord, there are people swallowers, too.

I think I have encountered a few of them in my lifetime—people who tried to swallow me whole—heart, soul and mind. Fighting daily, they oppressed me.

But I know today that I am especially fortunate because my husband is a Christian. I am grateful that *he* does not oppose the Christian way. He is a help and source of encouragement to me and together we "run the Christian race."

My prayer today is that You will comfort and give strength and wisdom to the Christian wives whose unsaved husbands are fighting the Christian way—husbands who *daily* oppress them. And help husbands who are trying to live Christian lives in homes with rebellious wives.

Be merciful, O God, to those Christians who struggle under this "daily oppression."

When God drew up the plans for this little town (as I am sure He must have, for it is such a lovely place!) He sketched tall elm trees along wide streets. He set an ocean at the edge of town, and shook out a white, laughing falls in the middle of the river. He placed chalk-white churches under the trees, and big rocks in the river for the water to wind around. And He made wide, friendly fields for the train to shout across.

He pulled the sky down close over the town—like a big, blue cap over a little boy's ears—and He painted the sky just the right shade of blue so the smoke would show in winter as it climbed up from the chimneys. He fixed the hills so they would send back echoes when the children shouted, and He put the river in a place where the children could walk to it and go skating.

He placed this town carefully, as He made the plans, in a section where snow would fall and cover it, and He made evergreen trees to catch the glistening flakes so the town would look like Christmas all through the winter. He placed the town in Maine where there would be red leaves to fill deep gutters so a child could go crackling through the leaves on a red-gold, autumn day.

In His mind God drew up the sketch . . . and saw that it was good . . . even before we were born. He said, "Let it be so" . . . and it was so!

Thank You, Lord, for Your foresight and Your delightful planning!

I remind myself of that statue of Atlas who carries the weight of the world on his shoulders. I take everything so *seriously*, Lord—the bad news in the daily paper, the deaths in the obituary column, the personal problems of friends, and my work.

I cannot see the sun for the obliterating clouds and smog. Help me to realize daily that I am *not* Atlas, that I am to cast my care upon You because You are stronger, more powerful and capable than I, or a million Atlases!

I read in the Bible today those cheerful words that "a merry heart doeth good like a medicine" (Prov. 17:22). I feel that a merry heart perhaps is a wholesome, rather carefree person who *is* concerned about problems but has prayed and has *transferred* the problems with their outcomes to You, which helps the person to face each day with courage, faith, and optimism.

Help me to cultivate the light heart so I can go happily through life knowing that "all things [do indeed] work together for good to them that love God, to them who are the called according to his purpose." And help me to realize that my part is prayer and commitment, and Yours is the responsibility for the outcome.

This morning I read in Psalm 106, verse 3, the words, "Blessed [is] . . . he that doeth righteousness at all times."

At *all* times! When the doorbell shrills, the kettle on the stove boils over, and the dog gets in the way. To "do righteousness" at 6:30 in the morning on an empty stomach when morale lags and the outlook is fuzzy.

To "do righteousness" when the children's incessant questions drive one up the wall, when the body is fatigued to the collapsing point, and the mind is boggled to the nth degree. When the rumor being spread about you is untrue. When your best friend lets you down. On those days when the mud of March clings to your boots and the burden of living clings to your soul.

At *all* times, do righteousness. Victoriously! Christ made it *possible.*

Get up, my soul, from your knees in the mud of March and lift up your head to the spring of April, and to the resurrected life of Christ, for He said, "My grace is sufficient for thee," and we have access to that marvelous, helpful grace through prayer!